A Kid's Guide to Drawing™

How to Draw
Cats

Laura Murawski

The Rosen Publishing Group's
PowerKids Press™
New York

Published in 2001 by The Rosen Publishing Group, Inc.
29 East 21st Street, New York, NY 10010

First Edition

Book Design: Kim Sonsky

Illustration Credits: Laura Murawski

Photo Credits: Title page by Thaddeus Harden; p. 6 © The Granger Collection; p. 8 © Everett Collection, Inc.; p. 10 © Tom McHugh/California Academy of Sciences; p. 12 © Henry Ausloos/Animals Animals; p. 16 © Robert Pearcy/Animals Animals; p. 18 © Robert Pearcy/Animals Animals; p. 20 © Superstock; p. 22 © Gerard Lacz/Animals Animals.

Manufactured in the United States of America

CONTENTS

1	Getting Started	4
2	The Goddess Bastet	6
3	Morris the Cat	8
4	The Saber-Toothed Cat	10
5	The Sphynx	12
6	The Siamese Cat	14
7	The Manx	16
8	The Kitten	18
9	The Black Cat	20
	Drawing Terms	22
	Glossary	23
	Index	24
	Web Sites	24

Getting Started

Learning how to draw cats is simple and fun! Do you have a cat as a pet? Have you ever wanted to own one but were unsure about which kind of cat to get? In this book, you'll learn about eight different types of cats. The domestic, or household, **breeds** are very different from one another. The shorthaired cat, for example, is believed to have come from a **species** of African wildcat. These wildcats were tamed by the ancient Egyptians more than 4,500 years ago. Longhaired cats, though, may have come from the Asian wildcat. The saber-toothed cat, which you will learn how to draw, is an **extinct** cat. It lived more than 20 million years ago and had a pair of huge, bladelike teeth. Today's Siamese cat has sharp teeth, too. Its teeth are used for biting rather than for stabbing and slashing its **prey**.

The supplies you will need to draw cats are:
- A sketch pad
- A number 2 pencil
- A pencil sharpener
- An eraser

Learning how to draw cats is a lot easier than you might think. Most of the drawings begin with circles and ovals. Some of the drawing terms, such as angular shapes and shade in, might be new to you. In the part called Drawing Terms, on page 22, you can find these terms. There are illustrations showing you what they look like to help you out.

The first drawing you will learn to do is that of the cat goddess Bastet. She was very popular with the Egyptians, who built a temple to honor her. You will learn how to draw Bastet in six steps. First you will draw circles and then you will connect them with lines. Beneath the drawings there are directions to help you through the steps. Each new step is shown in color to help guide you.

To draw cats, use the four Ps. These are **Patience**, **Persistence**, Practice, and a Positive **attitude**. Before you begin, try to find a quiet, clean, and well-lit space where you can pay attention to your drawing. Have fun, and good luck! Now, sharpen your pencils and let's pounce!

The Goddess Bastet

Lions and cats were **worshiped** in ancient Egypt. There was even an Egyptian goddess that people thought took the form of a cat. Her name was Bastet. She was thought to have special powers, including protecting mothers when they gave birth to their babies. Bastet also protected babies and children against dangerous animals and illnesses. She was also the goddess of music and dance. To honor her, the Egyptians built a huge temple in a place called Bubastis. When people came to worship Bastet at her temple they brought mummified cats to bury nearby. These dead cats had been treated with special chemicals to keep them from rotting. Egyptians also wore small figures of cats as necklaces or made statues of cats in bronze, a yellowish metal, to protect them from evil.

1

Draw two <u>circles</u>. Then draw a large <u>oval</u> crossing the bottom circle. Notice where the different shapes are placed. These shapes will form the body of Bastet.

2

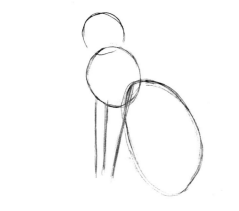

Next, draw three straight lines out from the middle circle. These will form the front legs.

3

Begin the cat's face by drawing part of a rectangle out from the left of the top circle. Draw an <u>angular shape</u> at the bottom of the three leg lines. This will make paws. Add another part of a rectangle at the bottom of the large oval.

4

Draw <u>curved lines</u> to make the front of the neck, the front paws, and the back paws. Add a straight line to join the first and second circles to make the back of the neck.

5

Add ears to the top circle. Curve the lines at the front of the face. Add a "t" as a guide for the rest of the face. Add a small curved line to the back of the shoulders. For the tail, add two curved lines at the bottom of the drawing.

6

Let's finish the drawing. Using the "t" guide, draw an eye, the mouth, and the nose. Add lines in the paws for the toes. Erase any extra lines.

7

Morris the Cat

Morris is one of the most popular shorthaired cats in America. You might remember him from his television ads for 9 Lives Cat Food. **Finicky** Morris has done many things besides television ads. He has appeared on many talk shows, including *Oprah Winfrey* and *Sally Jessy Raphael*. He has even been featured in magazines. Morris is listed as the author for three books about cats and cat health care. Even though he is famous, he is not a fancy breed of cat. Morris is an American shorthaired tabby, and the color of **marmalade**. The first Morris was discovered in 1968, in an animal shelter outside Chicago, Illinois. In all, there have been three Morrises. The most recent one was found in 1996!

1

Draw three circles. Make them larger in size from the top to the bottom. Notice how the two larger circles cross each other.

2

Join the small and medium circles by drawing two lines. For the front legs, add two angular shapes as shown.

3

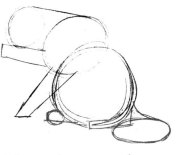

For the back legs, draw two shapes on the bottom of the large circle. Draw a small oval to make the tail and connect it to the large circle with a curved line.

4

Join the medium and large circles by making a curved line. Add the shapes like rounded triangles for ears on top of the small circle. Draw two lines in the shape of a "t" to serve as a guide for the face.

5

Using the "t" lines as a guide, draw eyes, the nose, and the tongue of Morris the cat. Draw a curved line between the rear ear and the middle circle to make the shoulders.

6

For whiskers, add a few curved lines as shown. Draw four small circles around a larger circle on the paw of the raised leg. These are called pads. Add curved lines for the toes and smaller ones for claws.

7

Now shade in your drawing. Look at the overall striped pattern of Morris's coat. By controlling the direction of the shading around his body you can create the feeling of fur. Great! You just drew Morris cleaning himself!

The Saber-Toothed Cat

The saber-toothed cat lived in the **Cenozoic era**, more than 20 million years ago. The saber-toothed cat is now extinct. Larger than today's lions, saber-tooths were named for the two long, curved, sharp teeth that grew from their upper jaw. Saber-tooths used these teeth to bite through the flesh of their prey. In North America, they probably hunted **bison** and **mastodons**. Most scientists believe that large saber-tooths walked flat-footed, like bears, not like today's cats. Scientists also think that saber-tooths became extinct when their main source of food, mastodons, died out over a million years ago.

1

Begin by drawing a large oval. This is the body. Add a smaller oval to the left. Draw it crossing the first oval. This is the head.

2

Next, draw two <u>rectangular shapes</u> beneath the body. Notice how one rectangular shape goes away from the body at an angle.

3

You're doing great! Now draw two angular shapes behind the rectangular shapes. You just drew the legs of the saber-toothed cat!

4

Draw curved lines at the top of the large circle to shape the back. Add a curved line to form the chest. For the tail, draw a "U" on its side. Add curved lines to the legs and head. Inside the head, draw a "t."

5

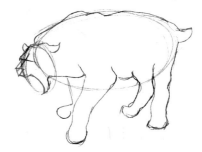

Now shape the head and face. Draw the ears, the nose, and the mouth, which is opened wide. Use the "t" to help you place the nose. Notice how the nose looks like a tiny triangle and the mouth looks like a backward "C."

6

You're doing great! Draw another backward "C" inside the one you already have. Connect the two "Cs" with a line to form the bottom of the opened mouth. For the two front teeth, add two curved, pointed shapes.

7

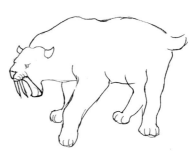

Finish your drawing by adding a <u>semicircle</u> for an eye, curved lines for whiskers, and curved lines in the paws for the toes. Erase any extra lines. You're done!

The Sphynx

The Sphynx is a modern cat. The first Sphynx was born in 1966, in Ontario, Canada. It is a very strange-looking cat because it has very little hair. It is not totally hairless, though. Its hair is just very short. Some people say that when they touch a Sphynx, it feels like a peach. It makes a great pet for people who have **allergies**. This is because when people are allergic to cats, it is usually the dander from the hair that is the problem. Other **characteristics** of the Sphynx are its loose and wrinkled skin, its large ears, and the way it stands with one front paw off the ground. The Sphynx got its name from the ancient Greek word *sphinx*. In Greek **myths**, a sphinx was a winged monster with a woman's head and a lion's body.

1

Draw two ovals, one large and one small. Notice where they are placed.

2

Now connect the two ovals by drawing two curved lines.

3

Next, add the front legs by drawing two sets of curved lines from the large oval. Join each set of lines with a straight line at the bottom.

4

For the back legs, add two angular shapes at the bottom of the large oval as shown.

5

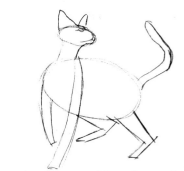

For the tail, draw two curved lines and join them. Add two triangles at the top for ears. Add two lines as guides for the nose and eyes.

6

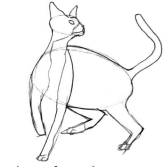

Now draw the face. Add a shape for an eye. Draw a tiny upside-down triangle for the nose.

7

Draw a line down from the nose on each side of the face. Add curved lines to make the paws. Join and curve all the lines.

8

Erase extra lines. Shade in the drawing.

13

The Siamese Cat

The Siamese cat first came from the Asian country of Thailand. Thailand used to be called Siam. The Siamese cat has a long, thin body and shiny fur. Its head is shaped like a triangle and its eyes slant toward its nose. It has great jumping ability and a very loud voice. The Siamese is born nearly all white, and has blue eyes. As it gets older, it gets darker shades of color in certain areas of its body. The temperature of the place where it is raised affects the color of its fur. The warmer the temperature, the lighter in color its fur will be. You will be drawing a Cream Point Siamese. Notice the way it is standing. It looks like it is **stalking** its prey. The back part of its body is raised, with its tail standing up straight.

Draw two small ovals and one much bigger oval. Notice how one of the small ovals crosses the bigger oval.

2

Now connect the ovals with three lines.

3

Add the tail by drawing a tall, curved shape from the top left of the biggest oval.

4

Now draw the back legs by making two angular shapes beneath the biggest oval.

5

Next, draw the front legs by making two more angular shapes at the other end of the big oval.

6

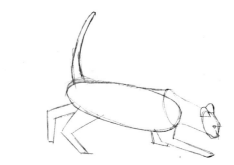

Draw two triangles with rounded tops for the ears at the top of the smallest oval. Add a "t" to the face to act as a guide for the next step.

7

Draw an eye, the nose, and the mouth using the "t" guide.

8

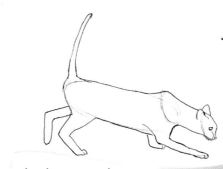

Curve the lines, and erase any extra ones.

The Manx

The Manx has no tail, or else it might have only the stump of one. Some Manx kittens are born with stumps of tails. Others are born with no tail at all. The Manx also has back legs that are much longer than its front ones. This causes the Manx to hop like a rabbit. In the 1600s, the Manx came from the Isle of Man, which is off the northwest coast of England. It is said that sailors brought this cat with them on trading ships to kill mice and rats on board. There is a Bible story about why the Manx does not have a tail. The story says that when Noah brought animals onto the ark before the flood, the Manx cat got its tail stuck in the ark's door when it closed. Scientists, though, believe the Manx is tailless because it has a **genetic defect**. They think the tail does not form as it should.

1

Begin by drawing two circles and one small oval. Notice where they are placed.

2

Now connect the circles by drawing four lines as shown.

3

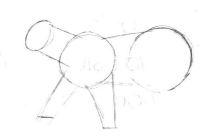

Draw the front legs by adding two angular shapes below the middle circle.

4

Draw the back legs by adding two more angular shapes below the circle at the right.

5

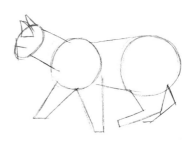

Draw the ears by adding two triangular shapes to the small oval. Add a "t" to the front to act as a guide for the next step.

6

Draw an eye, the nose, and the mouth using the "t" as a guide.

7

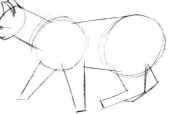

Connect and curve all the lines in your drawing. Add a tiny bump where a tail would be.

8

Shade in the striped pattern of the fur.

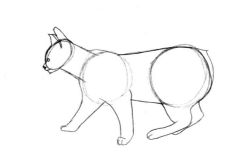

The Kitten

The little kitten you will draw here is practicing a very important way to hunt. This way of hunting is called the Bird Swat, and the kitten is doing a great job even though it is only six weeks old! There are two other methods used in hunting. The kitten will learn these by the time it is nine weeks old. They are the Mouse Pounce and the Fish Scoop. In the Mouse Pounce, the kitten leaps sideways and then springs down on its prey. In the Fish Scoop, it makes a flipping motion as its claws get ready to toss the fish out of the water. By about 12 weeks, most kittens are able to hunt as well as most adult cats can.

1

Draw a long oval and then two circles at the top and bottom that cross the oval.

2

Draw two pairs of curved lines. One pair goes up from the oval and one goes down.

3

Now draw two little circles at the bottom of the oval. Add a curved shape to make the hind paw of the kitten.

4

Draw the triangular ears. For the tail, add a "C" shape on the left side of the circle.

5

Add lines to shape the back. Also curve the lines of the front legs and paws. Add a "t" to the face to be a guide later. Add the yarn.

6

Finish the face by making a small triangle for the nose, two small ovals for the eyes, and lines for the mouth. Add lines for the toes.

7

Erase extra lines. Finish the paws, eyes, and nose. Add lines in the ears and on the face for hair.

The Black Cat

There are many myths about black cats. One is that if you see a black cat cross your path it means you will have bad luck. During Halloween you probably see many decorations and costumes that include a black cat with its back arched. How did the black cat come to mean bad luck? In many societies, the color black is connected to death and illness. Most likely the black-cat myth came from Europe in the **Middle Ages**. It was believed that a witch would sometimes take the shape of a black cat. The black cat was thought to be evil and dangerous. The fact that cats like to walk around and hunt at night only added to the scariness of the black cat.

1

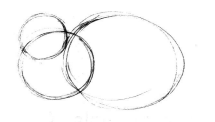

Begin by drawing three circles of different sizes. Notice where they cross each other.

2

Next, draw a tiny circle and a rectangular shape at the bottom of the middle circle. You just made the front leg and paws.

3

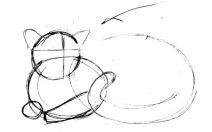

Draw the ears at the top of the upper circle. For the tail, add two curved lines to the larger circle as shown. Draw a "t" in the face to act as a guide for the next steps.

4

Add a curve to join the head to the body. Curve the lines for the front paw and leg. Using the "t" guide, add the eyes and nose.

5

Very good! Now let's draw the opened mouth. Draw a rectangle below the nose. Add a triangle on its side to the left of the rectangle.

6

Now draw the teeth by making four pointed shapes at each corner of the rectangle. Add curved lines for the whiskers near the nose. Draw curved lines on the paws to make the toes.

7

Erase any extra lines. Shade in the mouth, the eyes, and the nose. Shade in the fur if you want to make the scary cat all black!

Drawing Terms

These are some of the words and shapes you need to know to draw cats:

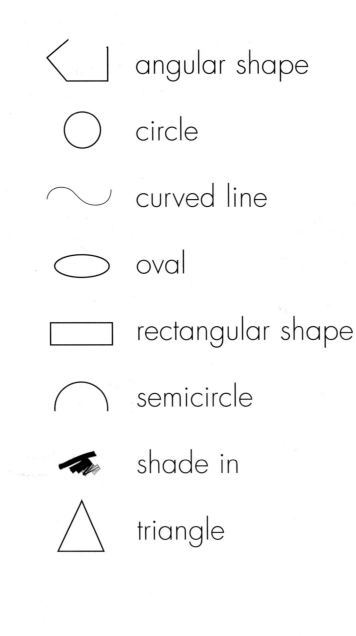

angular shape

circle

curved line

oval

rectangular shape

semicircle

shade in

triangle

Glossary

allergies (AH-lur-jeez) Bad reactions to certain things, such as animals or pollen.

attitude (AH-tih-tood) A person's outlook or position toward a fact or situation.

bison (BY-zin) A wild animal of North America, related to cattle, with a shaggy head and a hump above its shoulders. Also called buffalo.

breeds (BREEDS) Groups of animals that look very much alike and have the same kind of relatives.

Cenozoic era (se-neh-ZOH-ik IR-ah) A period of history that includes the Tertiary and Quarternary periods, from about 65 million years ago to the present time. It is the time when mammals, birds, plants, modern continents, and glaciers developed.

characteristics (kar-ek-ter-IS-tiks) Features that make something or someone special.

extinct (ik-STINKT) No longer in existence.

finicky (FIH-nih-kee) Being very choosy or fussy about one's taste.

genetic defect (jih-NEH-tik DEE-fekt) A problem that causes a person's or animal's body to develop differently than it normally would.

marmalade (MAR-meh-layd) A jamlike spread that is made from oranges or other fruit. The color of marmalade is usually orange.

mastodons (MAS-tuh-dons) Distant prehistoric relatives of the elephant.

Middle Ages (MID-dul AY-jes) The period in European history between ancient and modern times, from about 500 A.D. to about 1450.

myths (MITHS) Stories that people make up to explain events in nature or in history.

patience (PAY-shunts) The ability to wait calmly for something.

persistence (per-SIS-tehns) The ability to continue to do something without giving up.

prey (PRAY) An animal that is eaten by another animal for food.

species (SPEE-sheez) A group of living things that have certain basic things in common.

stalking (STAWK-ing) Following something closely and secretly.

worshiped (WUR-shipt) To have paid great honor or respect to something or someone.

Index

A
American shorthaired
    tabby, 8

B
Bastet, 5, 6
Bible, 16
Bird Swat, 18
black cat, 20

C
Cenozoic era, 10
Cream Point Siamese,
    14

F
Fish Scoop, 18

H
Halloween, 20

K
kitten, 18

M
Manx, 16
mastodons, 10
Middle Ages, 20
Morris the cat, 8
Mouse Pounce, 18

N
9 Lives Cat Food, 8

O
Oprah Winfrey, 8

S
saber-toothed cat, 4,
    10
Sally Jessy Raphael, 8
Siamese, 4, 14
Sphynx, 12

Web Sites

Due to the changing nature of Internet links, PowerKids Press has developed an online list of Web sites related to the subject of this book. This site is updated regularly. Please use this link to access the list:
www.powerkidslinks.com/kgd/cats/